MY TITHE AND MY BLESSINGS

Hezekiah Vincent O. Asa

My Tithe And My Blessings

Unless otherwise stated, all scriptures quotations are taken from the King James Version of the Holy Bible.

ISBN: 979-850-841-432-0

Published and Printed in Nigeria by:
Living Christ Ambassadors Assembly for
Ambassadors Hall Publication

ambassadorshall@gmail.com
ambassadorshall@yahoo.com
20 Noah Omoboye Street, off Mopo Road
United Estate Sangotedo Eti-Osa, Lagos State Nigeria.
08177017460, 08121594694, 08035516360

Dedication

I dedicate this book to every true child of God and disciples of Jesus Christ, who are ready to follow to the very end in obedience. Also, I recognise all the preachers of the gospel of Christ in pureness and righteousness, who are also upholding the word in wholesomeness.

I also dedicate this to my dear wife, **Deborah M. A. Asa,** for all her prayers and show of love for what I am called to do. To Pastor Joel Obikoru, Pastor Collins Hezekiah Vincent and to all my children in the faith. I say, may God bless you all in Christ Jesus name.

Acknowledgment

But we speak the wisdom of God in a mystery, even the hidden wisdom, which God ordained before the world unto our glory.

1 Corinthians 2:7

Our God be praised for His wisdom and revelation knowledge in putting together various parchments in the making of this book.

To Jesus Christ, the great high Priest, and the Holy Spirit, the Revealer; both have released the divine direction with a deep understanding of this uncommon topic. The issue of Tithing has turned many believers from a scriptural injunction, there decoding it as a crucial and multifaceted problem. Its teaching today has caused cracks in Christendom.

Many thanks to all the Pastors and other ministers that God has used to encourage this race, and the wisdom which they have used in one way or the other to push this work. Their physical and spiritual contributions have, in no small measure, helped to shapen the outcome of this book.

My gratitude also goes to all members of the Living Christ Ambassadors Assembly for their continued efforts to see that things work according to the will and purpose of God. My God will never forget their good work in Christ Jesus.

God be glorified forever and ever – Amen.

Contents

Introduction

It is getting to the time that disciples of Christ wil earnestly commit themselves to the word of God, like the children of Israel did.

> ***And they answered Joshua, saying, All that thou commandest us we will do, and whithersoever thou sendest us, we will go. According as we hearkened unto Moses in all things, so will we hearken unto thee: only the Lord thy God be with thee, as he was with Moses.***
>
> Joshua 1:16-1

It is time to start looking critically at God's word an doing just what it says without asking why. The reward o following God's word is not to God, but us. Nothing sha the Lord lose as it were if we fail to hear and do His will, bu we stand to throw away everything that would hav benefited our lives and become what He created us to b from the foundation of human race.

Everything we do in life is guided by one principle or th other; nothing happens by accident. The life we live, w live by the principles of the one that has made life possible, and without him, nothing works appropriately on earth's surface. He owns all things, build all things, and directs all things. We are what we are because He has commanded it to be so.

By commandment, God has allowed men to take charge of the earth He made with all its pleasure. But in taking care of the world, men must not lose sight of God's word, because all other forces that contend with man are obedient to God's word. The Lord has said, “I have made all things to work together for your good”. Whenever we display good inside of us, we attract His goodwill that is made available towards all men.

To effectively do the will of God, you need Jesus Christ, who is the word himself to control your affairs. Many today do not have Him; that is why it is effortless for them to flout God's order at the slightest provocation. Learn to follow God like a child, and it will be a simple thing to carry out His instructions any time without thinking how the flesh receives it.

Tithing and other Christian ordinances are easily disregarded in our present generation due to so many adulterated teachings that have gotten believers confused about what and whom to believe. According to the scripture, man has increased in knowledge which leads to grief and sorrow. So many Christians now place more trust in men than hold onto the word of God.

The issue of tithing has turned many believers from basic scriptural injunction and now decoding tithe as a crucial and multifaceted problem. It's a teaching in this present age that has caused so much cracks in Christendom.

Failing to do what God is saying in His word is disobedience to His will. One can never be deemed right with God if His word is not in that individual's life. It is this word in our lives that gives direction on how best we can live to glorify God. Each of God's law we keep and continue to practice points and draws us nearer to God. Blessings are cheap when we are walking within the purview of the governing rules of God.

If we can do well to follow as the Lord desires every man to do, we shall all rejoice in His presence every single hour with Him here on earth and also in glory when we meet with Him – Halleluiah.

Chapter 1

ABRAHAM AND MELCHIZEDEK

Abraham was already in the heart of God as the best choice in reaching out to all nations of the earth before he was called to leave his country, kindred, and the father's house. God saw in Abraham what He wanted to do with man, and then He started leading him step after step to get to the destination that would bring blessing to all flesh. Because God had excellent plans for man, He took Abraham as the starting point to put in him what He intends for all people of the world.

Our God is wonderful. He knows what He wants and more than a thousand ways on how to go about whatever He intends to achieve. God is never constrained by time, seasons, or man's ideas. The blessings and the fulfillment of the humans on earth are packaged by God in one man, Abraham.

Tithing is one of many means that the father intends to bless the children of men, and this He impressed into the heart of Abraham as an example for everyone that shall come after him.

Honestly speaking, the issue of tithe precedes the Mosaic Law. It was exemplified in Abraham and affirmed by our Lord Jesus Christ during his earthly ministration. The scriptures made it clear that tithe does not belong to the giver, but God.

> **And all the tithe of the land, whether of the seed of the land or the fruit of the tree, is the Lord's; it is holy unto the Lord.**
>
> Leviticus 27:30

God has, through His commandment, instructed the Israelites to make sure they do not touch the tenth part which He kept for Himself. So, it was necessary that the tenth portion, which is known as the tithe, be brought to the storehouse for ministerial work.

Abraham was God's beloved because he learned to follow God the way he is directed. Abraham never questioned God on anything, but as he hears, he observes, and the result of his humble act was wonderful.

When Abraham was on his way from the slaughter of Chedorlaomer (the King of Elam), the first King that met him was the King of Sodom, who congratulated Abraham for his victory. Abraham left the King of Sodom to meet Melchizedek, King of Salem, who brought forth bread and wine to him. This King of Salem the Bible says is a priest of the Most High God.

> **Without father or mother, descent, having neither beginning of days, nor end of life, but like unto the Son of God; abideth a priest continually.**
>
> Hebrew 7:3

Melchizedek blessed Abraham with the heavenly blessings, which created a great cover and gave him the power to reign over his enemies. And in return, Abraham gave a tithe of all out of the booty he got from Elam to fulfil the principle of the tenth portion commanded by God. He knew by the nature of God in him that the tithe belongs to God, and he will not want to offend the Lord in this wise.

Abraham's commitment towards the Lord was not jus in some areas but in all of God's laws and instructions. He will instead wave man aside than turning blind eyes ove the matters that pertain to God-man relationship. Thi patriarch knows how to please the Lord of his soul.

How much of God's word can you carry to heart as a Christian whose trust is absolute? Abraham's love for God never changed from what it used to be, starting from the day God called him out to serve; else he would have submitted the tenth portion (tithe) to the King he first met (the King of Sodom) instead of Melchizedek, the King of peace and righteousness.

Melchizedek stood in the place of the Son of God, while Abraham became the example that man should follow to know the mind of God. Abraham discovered that meeting the King of Salem was going to bring something good, but more so, he was convinced that this personality is not an ordinary man.

Abraham knew by the Spirit that this man a special being sent from God, and so, he gave what rightfully is God's. Melchizedek blessed Abraham after giving him the bread and wine, then Abraham, in turn, gave him "tithe of all" (Genesis 14:18-20). There is enough blessing in tithing already proclaimed by God, and those that pay tithe only succeeded in walking into the pool of blessings.

A man of God once testified and said he decided to try God's word on tithe and started paying his tithe accurately. Over time, he began to experience changes in his finance, and as a result of this, he increased it by another ten percent.

As he continued to see a constant increase financially and in every area of life, he changed the twenty percent to ninety percent for God and reserved ten percent for himself. According to him, the change benefited him beyond measure even with 10% only. No one enters a deal with God and gets frustrated at the end.

Child of God, "nothing endures but changes; day by day, what you do is who you become. Your integrity is your destiny. It is the light that guides your way" – Heraclitus.

Abraham believed God's word and kept bringing the part that is due to God when it was time to do so. The Lord God also did not fail in blessing Him, because that is what has been written concerning the payment of tithe. If you find that things are not working right since you have been holding back your tithe from God, change and start paying it. Prove Him according to what He said in His word:

> **....If I will not open you the windows of heaven, and pour you out a blessing, that there shall not be room enough to receive it.**
>
> Malachi 3:10.

The reason why some people are running up and down

is that they are not convinced that God is able and can entirely do what He says He will do. God is not just willing to bless; He can bless and help you in all things.

Beloved, those who say, "if I perish, I perish," never perish because they are convinced that even when they pay that tithe with all they have at hand, God will not allow them to beg for bread. Your life, goods, and treasures should be directed towards the kingdom of God so that you can have a storehouse that thieves never can break into and steal.

> **Lay not up for yourselves treasures upon earth, where moth and rust doth corrupt, and where thieves break through and steal; But lay up for yourselves treasures in heaven, where neither moth nor rust doth corrupt and where thieves do not break through nor steal: for where your treasure is, there will your heart be also.**

Mathews 6:19-21.

The tithe and other givings were always coming from Abraham's bowel, which secured lasting treasure for him, his children, and his children-children.

The extension of Abraham's benevolence gave rise to the blessings that all the nations of the world enjoy today. Paying of the tithe is not an order from Abraham; it is from God who said, "give me the tenth part it's mine; if you take it, you are robbing me."

Abraham knew that God is faithful to His Word, and so he taught Isaac to give the tithe. Isaac passed it on to Jacob, and down the line, the practice of the law continued from one generation to the other.

MELCHIZEDEK

Melchizedek occupies the dual office of both King and priest of the Most High God, an office we will later see Jesus Christ occupy.

> **And Melchizedek king of Salem brought forth bread and wine, and he was the priest of the most high God**
>
> Genesis 14:18

Melchizedek strengthened Abraham with the bread and wine he gave to him after such an energy-sapping battle he just won. But there was more to the link between Abraham and Melchizedek that we need to know here.

This Melchizedek was not only a king but the King of Peace and Priest directly from God whom the scripture says he is made like unto the son of God. He has all the qualities of the Lord, our Saviour Jesus Christ.

> **Now consider how great this man was, unto whom even the patriarch Abraham gave the tenth of the spoils**
>
> Hebrews 7:4

As the Levitical priesthood, which was being operated by men and ordained through the instructions of God to handle matters concerning the law, received tithes, they also paid tithes from what they were getting from the people.

So, this priesthood was the perfect one that was imperfect until it was made perfect and blessed through Christ who came in the order of Melchizedek. The King of righteousness blessed Abraham and took a tithe of all (the tenth part) from him, and as part of Abraham's blessings, so, we must be part of his obedience.

Child of God know this: your tithe carries a blessing before it leaves your hand to God. The blessing that Melchizedek released onto Abraham before receiving tithe from him also runs in the families of the earth that follows the footstep of this humble and faithful father of faith.

Your tithe has a connection to the level of what flows into you as the windows of heaven are opened to bless. There will always be a blessing by whatever thing you have done right, or things done according to scripture Melchizedek is the source of the blessing that goes with the payment of tithe, and the Bible says he is, “Made like unto the Son of God which abideth a priest forever” (Hebrew 7:3b).

Jesus came after the similitude of Melchizedek, who is an eternal priest with the power of everlasting life. It is this supernatural nature that Jesus came with to live amongst us that gave Him authority and power to affirm all the commandments of the father, which includes tithe.

Jesus has a testimony all over the Christian religious world that he is the only known High Priest forever after the order of Melchizedek (Hebrews 7:17 NLT).

> **And the Psalmist pointed this out when he said of Christ, “You are a priest forever in the line of Melchizedek.”**

ABRAHAM AND MELCHIZEDEK

Chapter 2

THE TENTH PART OF ALL

The principle of tithing the tenth portion dates to the time of Adam and Eve in the garden of Eden. In Genesis chapter number three, God has placed the first family in the garden of Eden to dress and take care of it. All that they needed to enjoy life were provided in the garden, but even so, there remaineth a reserved portion by God as a forbidden area for Adam and Eve.

This principle of the tenth portion later resonated with Abraham, when he met Melchizedek, the King of Salem. Abraham was coming from the slaughter and met first with the King of Sodom and then Melchizedek, King of Salem who served him bread and wine.

The Bible recorded that Melchizedek was the priest of the Most High God. He blessed Abraham as directed from above by the most High God, the possessor of heaven and earth, and Abraham gave a tithe of all.

Genesis 14:17-18

> ***And the king of Sodom went out to meet him, after his return from the slaughter of Chedorlaomer, and of the kings that were with him, at the valley of Shaveh, which in the king's dale.***
>
> ***And Melchizedek king of Salem brought forth bread and wine: and he was the priest of the Most High God. "And he blessed him, and said, Blessed be Abram of the most high God, possessor of heaven and earth: And blessed be the most high God, which hath delivered thine enemies into thy hand. And he gave him tithes of all".***

God was pleased by Abraham's obedience to the principle concerning the tenth portion because he feared and submitted to God instead of the devil in likeness of the King of Sodom. God showed up and assured him of His all-round protection and provision toward him and his seed.

> ***I am thy shield and thy exceeding great reward.***

Genesis 15:1.

Abraham established himself in God's blessings by releasing that portion that belongs to God without holding back. What Abraham did in the obedience of the word of God to be blessed extended to Isaac his Son. Isaac started enjoying the fruit of the father's obedience to God because at the period he faced opposition from the Philistines, the Lord appeared to him and said:

> ***Fear not, for I am with thee, I am going to bless you multiply your seed because of my servant Abraham.***
>
> *Genesis 26:24*

The keeping of the tenth portion principle has a memorial backup. Abraham kept the commandment, and Isaac, his son, reaped from it. The principle of the tenth part has a long-lasting gathering. One made the sacrifice, and the other benefited from it.

I can see the continuation of this principle in the life of Isaac and his son(s). Abraham died after a fulfilled life in God and Isaac, his son, took on the grace of the father's blessings. There are blessings tied to observance of the principle of the tenth portion and transferred blessings also.

Isaac grew old, and the Bible says, his eyes were becoming too dim to be able to see, and so he knew that death was around the corner. Due to this condition, Isaac called his eldest son and said:

> ***... behold now, I am old, I know not the day of my death, ... so go out to the field, and take me some venison, and make for me savory meat, such as I love, and bring it to me, that I may eat; that my soul may bless thee before I die***
>
> *Genesis 27:1-4*

Isaac said bring me this portion from all you will gather and set it before me that my soul may bless thee. We get blessed when what is released matches what is requested to provoke a blessing. It was the portion that Jacob later brought that caused Isaac to release blessing from the depth of his heart upon him.

> ***And he said, bring it near to me, and I will eat of my Son's venison, that my soul blesses thee. And he brought it near to him, and he did eat, and he brought him wine, and he***

drank. And his father Isaac said unto him, come near now, and kissed him ...see, the smell of my son is as the smell of a field which the Lord hath blessed.

Genesis 27:25-1

Isaac exemplified the principle of the tenth portion b his request for a portion of the venison, which Jaco provided to get the blessing. Jacob received the father' blessing and sojourned to Padan-aram where he started new life and prospered there.

He enjoyed the good of the land presented by God, an he never forgot the part that belongs to God, the tent part. Jacob recognised that his life is a product of God' help, so he vowed and made God his only source and wen ahead to declare:

... And of all that thou shall give me, I will surely give the tenth unto thee

Genesis 28:2

He followed the steps of his father and grandfather, an God was well pleased. Your observance of this princip has great benefits to you and, by extension, your busines children, and children's children if they follow.

The principle of the tenth part can work for anyone that applies the rule without distortion. Never you listen to people who say the payment of tithe is not of God or unscriptural. This principle is of God, and it is workable according to laid down guidelines.

Chapter 3

TITHE IS A COMMANDMENT

God came up with a system where the priests and Levites can be supported so that they do not go hungry as they carry out the functions of their God-given assignments. They are not to work in the fields, but in the house of God to stand for the whole of Israel.

The duty of atoning and making of prayers for sin was placed on the priests. And the collection of tithes from the rest of them is regarded as working in their field. It is the way God Himself defines it. They are God's workers maintaining and overseeing the activities of God in the field on behalf of the Lord who has hired them. When they gather their produce or earn income together and then shared into ten parts, one of the parts is reserved for God's ministers and the sanctuary.

God declared that this tenth portion which is for Him; He has given to the children of Levi for an inheritance. Why? Because they have no other work except the one assigned to them by God. "And, behold, I have given the children of Levi all the tenth in Israel for an inheritance, for their service which they serve, even the service of the tabernacle of the congregation" (Num. 18:21).

God has given this order from the beginning, and since then, He has not countered it. The children of Israel have followed the commandment to date. Know this: where there is no produce from the field, money is used instead. The Priest and Levites are the ministers, Pastors, Apostles, and Bishops of today's church.

What does your service to God as a child or believer entails if not to cleave unto Him and serve Him with all your heart and all your soul?

Joshua gave a charge to the Reubenites, Gadites, and the half-tribe of Manasseh that they should hold onto the commandment and the law as instructed by Moses. They were also to walk in the way of the Lord in love to keep all that has been commanded (Joshua 22:5).

In the church of today, we choose what we like to do and the way it will please us, and not how to impress God. There are areas of God's word that man wants to apply human wisdom and adopt our doctrine rather than following God. The reason is that if we take God's way, the people (congregation) will oppose us and may eventually leave the church. So, we feel it is good we do it the way of the people to retain them for a classic congregation.

God is not interested in how we feel when we do not take heed to His charge, but He will be more mindful of us if what we do is done according to His word.

God will not change His word because someone refuses to accept it. Beloved, a tithe is one of the many charges we must give heed to so that we can gain the attention of God in whatever thing we do in His name on earth.

Joshua got the tithes and offered what is due to God. He blessed the people after that and sent them away. Joshua was a doer of God's word, including his household.

God does not lie. When He says a thing, He brings it to pass because His word is "ye and amen." The scripture says of all the things the Lord promised the children of Israel to do, none failed. *"There failed not aught of any good thing which the Lord has spoken unto the house of Israel; all came to pass"* (Joshua 21:45).

So, it is for everyone that obeys Him in keeping His word in our present generation. If God says there is a blessing when you pay tithe, that is precisely the way it is, child of God.

TITHE IS LIFE, NOT DEATH

> **In the beginning, God created the heaven and the earth.**
>
> **Genesis 1:1**

Even in creation, God started from the beginning, and everything He set to do was with a purpose. When God called forth light and saw that it was good, He went ahead to divide the light from the darkness, which he saw inside it. The Bible says the light He called "Day and the darkness He called "Night". Then, the night and day are termed the evening and the morning, which is the first day.

Beloved, it is not in error for God to detail creation in distinct numerical expressions. He started from day one to seven, which is the day of His rest and went further to numeral number ten, which He has set aside for Himself to save man from death.

In the kingdom of our God, these numerical representations have their various meanings that will help us understand that the payment of tithe gives life and not death. Every one of the numbers (1-10) connotes everything that man needs to know as long as he lives. Man needs to know and understand the world he is in and appreciate the personality (the God) that has dropped him on earth. We are here for a purpose divinely designed by God, the creator.

NUMEROLOGY AND MEANING

Our God is good with the use of numbers when explaining certain issues as it concerns Himself and all His handiworks.

Let us consider some of these numerals:

Number		Meaning
1.	-	The unity of God
2.	-	Witness
3.	-	Power, Dominion, Influence
4.	-	Balance, Light, Stability
5.	-	Grace
6.	-	The number of man
7.	-	Perfection, Completion, Rest
8.	-	New beginning, Fresh start
9.	-	Prosperity, Multiplication, Fruitfulness
10.	-	Death, Extinction, Lost

Jesus Christ came to save the world from sin, pains, and death because He only has the power over death as the Bible has said, *"Knowing that Christ being raised from the dead dieth no more; death hath no more dominion over him" (Romans 6:9).*

Dearly beloved, you can see that from the numerological arrangement above, the last figure 10 means death, extinction, and loss which nobody will desire to keep. And as you can observe from number 1 to the last, it is only number 10 that any normal person would not want to associate with because it spells evil; something sinister, awful and woeful. Only an insane pesron will leave out dominion, God's grace, the sabal of God, prosperity, increase and then choose woe and death.

Now listen, child of God, when you give God the tenth portion, which is death, you gain life, power, balance, and the grace to prosper amid your enemies. Where your enemies are failing, you are going higher. Where they are crying and wailing, you are rejoicing and celebrating long life.

Giving away that part that God has power over grants you the opportunity to get a life first, and later, power over the number of man, and prosper because only the living man has the strength to pursue life jollies. No one pays tithe correctly to God and will not receive something in return. Note the verse of the scriptures that gave credence to tithing, then do as is written.

> **Bring ye all the tithes into the storehouse... and prove me now herewith, saith the Lord of hosts, if I will not open you the windows of heaven, and pour you out a blessing, that there shall not be room enough to receive it"**
>
> *Malachi 3:10.*

Tithing, according to the commandment, can cause miraculous doors to open for you where there were only walls.

A woman of God, Lisa Nichols, said, "you are the designer of your destiny. You are the author. You write the story. The pen is in your hand, and the outcome is whatever you choose." What then is your choice? Life or death.

EARNESTLY COMMITTED

The church of Jesus Christ is a place for practical experience of the blessings of tithing. A church that can religiously follow the command of tithing is a church prepared to prosper beyond the ordinary level. The children of God should always be encouraged to pay their tithe to God accurately, and His word will take effect in their lives.

The word of God, which says "...if I will not open you the windows of heaven, and pour you out a blessing, that there shall not be room enough to receive it" shows that He is waiting for those who will humbly do what will open the windows of heaven.

It's the responsibility of church leaders, pastors, and teachers to properly inform their congregants of the importance of paying tithe to God. The people are tied down from prospering if they hold back their tithes. They lose blessings not in one particular area of life but on all sides. Our blessings come by doing God's will, not our pleasurable personal will.

God said if you do this, I will do that. It is in your doing that the windows of heaven's blessings are made wide open. Many children of God don't put this to heart because they feel when they give the tithe, their finances will reduce, and money would be wasted. Child of God, your prosperity is based on your submission to the laws of God; do not forget this truth.

You need to realise that your local church where you get all the attention, care, prayers, and blessings must be maintained - equipment purchased, bills paid, and many other exigencies. The church has to be on the ground in a way that your needs can effectively be handled. And if paying your tithe and other financial commitments is too heavy for you, you do not wish the place you call home the best.

The tithe, offerings, and various contributions are key factors that reveal commitment and loyalty to your local assembly. The one getting value is one who earnestly seeks for the survival of where his gains emanate.

Chapter 4

TITHE IS GAIN NOT PAIN

Will a man rob God? Yet ye have robbed me. But ye say, wherein have we robbed thee? In tithes and offerings

Malachi 3:8.

This statement was from God rightfully accusing Israel of their act of sin by holding back the tithes and offering. Paying of tithes and offerings was commanded before the law handed over to Moses.

And blessed be the most high God, which hath delivered thin enemies into thy hand. And he gave him tithes of all.

Genesis 14:20.

It was enforced under grace by Jesus Christ.

Woe unto you, scribes and Pharisees, hypocrites! For ye pay tithe of mint and anise and cummin, and have omitted the weightier matters of law, judgment, mercy, and faith: these ought ye to have done, and not to leave the other undone.

Matthew 23:23

Israel moved from the part of obedience to disobeying God at will. This backsliding act of the nation caused them to go through so many pains and experiences that heavily put pressure on them until they were challenged by the Lord to prove Him with their tithes and offerings.

The payment of tithe and its twin sister, the offering, does not give pains to the giver but gain. Listen, child of God, the house and ministers of God are to be taken care of by those in the body of Christ (the believing Christians) who daily seek God in fellowship. The house of God never should suffer lack; that is why the Lord went all out to provide and bless all who call on Him.

The tithes and offerings that God's people bring to His house are what He breaths on to return the same to them for a blessing. Beloved, “a blessing” is heavier than blessings because a blessing is a source that sustains your blessings – glory to God. Release of your tithe triggers the source of your blessing for a continued flow of your blessings.

Often, I hear some people say there is no need anymore to pay tithe; it is Old Testament law; we are not under the law but grace. Hear what the scripture says concerning this deposition.

> **For sin shall not have dominion over you: for ye are not under the law but grace. What then? Shall we sin, because we are not under the law, but under grace? God forbid.**
>
> Romans 6:14-16

Hear this and do not be deceived by any man, not obeying God's command is disobedience, and every disobedience before God is sin and transgression of the law.

> **And Samuel said, Hath the Lord as great delight in burnt offerings and sacrifices, as in obeying the voice of the LORD? Behold, to obey is better than sacrifice, and to hearken than the fat of rams. For rebellion is as the sin**

> **of witchcraft, and stubbornness is as iniquity and idolatry. Because thou hast rejected the word of the Lord, he hath also rejected thee from being king.**
>
> *1 Samuel 15:22-23*

Many Christians take what they want to believe and leave the rest because it does not go down well with their head knowledge. The word of God is not about what you like or what you hate to accept; it has been commanded long before you because you are a believer.

In the real sense, it is to our credit as believers to observe all rules or regulations. But then, where anyone fails to obey the voice of God in certain areas as instructed, he or she is counted as a transgressor.

> **Whosoever committeth sin transgresseth also the law: for sin is the transgression of the law.**
>
> 1 John 3:4

Beloved, do not draw the pains of disregard for God's law by your modernity in response to what is going on in Christendom. Even though it is a time of grace, it is never a ticket for anyone to seek a personal foundation to start building on.

It is dangerous because the outcome can never be a perfect one. We as Christians are expected to build upon the foundation of the apostles and prophets which had Jesus Christ as the chief cornerstone (Ephesians 2:20).

What gain will be more required that when the creator Himself has said that as long as the earth remains, seedtime and harvest shall not cease (Genesis 8:22)? So, it is with every seed you sow (financial or otherwise) in the course of the gospel. It's bound to reproduce back to you multiple times. Each bountiful release from a cheerful heart brings generous returns anytime, anywhere, according to the mandate of the almighty God.

How do I know that tithing has gain and not pain? It's because God said so. He made all things by His sure word; none faileth. The same God has said, "prove me now herewith if I will not open you...."

From the time you start tithing and giving your offerings, four things begin to form around you.

The number one thing shall be enough meat in God's house that will eradicate lack, and His work not hindered anymore. Secondly, the windows of heaven will be made open to pour out a blessing that will greatly flow that no room enough to take all.

Thirdly, the Lord himself will drive away from you the enemy and destroyer of harvest (devourer), and the gain remains. And fourthly, He will make sure that all living shall acknowledge that of a truth, God has blessed you and made you a pleasurable one. These four rewards of tithing are what I called tithe gain.

TITHE IS STORED NOT WASTED

Never will anything placed in the hands of the Lord go missing; it is preserved, and a hundred percent secure. It is in the power of God to keep in safety every seed sown in His name. Tithe paid, vows, first fruit, and offerings given are all seed kept in store with God.

Though cash may be going out of your hands, that does not mean it's being wasted or thrown away, but kept with God to bring more harvest on a later date. Except a corn of wheat falls into the ground and die, it abides alone: but if it dies, it brings forth much fruit (John 12:24). The benefits of tithing are more to man than to God.

Beloved of the Lord, the ten per cent that God is asking from you is that portion of the ten percent He has blessed you with. This is the fraction that is called tithe that God is withholding to sustain your continued blessing. Paying it out ensures your every time storage. Tithing is storing and not wasting.

The Lord spoke to my spirit, saying:

> **There are so many of my children who still argue my word even with my miraculous acts in their lives: I will surprise many on the last day for their self-will: my word will not change because man has refused to take it to heart as to do what I have instructed. I have said it again and again, none of my word that had gone out of my mouth will come back to me void.**

Our God is ever committed to His Word, and without any doubt, every instruction or law from the Lord has two sides: if you keep any instruction, there is a blessing, and if you disregard an instruction, there is punishment. Then, it is your choice to go for a blessing or settle for punishment.

TITHE, A COVENANT PRINCIPLE

Everyone wants to be identified and linked to Abraham because God greatly blessed him to the knowledge of all humans. God has connected every man's blessings to father Abraham divinely, so children of Abraham in faith must have to walk in his steps. No believer has ever regretted being connected to the stock of Abraham literally (see Romans 4:12).

> **And the father of circumcision to them who are not of the circumcision only, but who also walk in the steps of that faith of our father Abraham, which he had being yet uncircumcised.**

Know this, even while Abraham was yet to be circumcised, he paid tithe to Melchizedek, and he, in turn, received the blessing. Tithing is proof of obedience and appreciation of the goodness of God towards man. We cannot quantify the blessings of tithing, but let's note some of these blessings that will enable us to take tithing more seriously:

1. Tithing connects you to God's light that brings the increase.
2. Tithing sets your helpers loose to locate you
3. Tithing lifts you from where you were to a higher and entirely new place
4. Tithing links you to long life
5. Tithing brings divine protection and constant provision

6. Tithing can end financial hindrance in your life
7. Tithing opens doors that even the devil couldn't shut against you
8. Tithing brings a constant flow of fruitfulness and exempts you from shame.
9. Tithing cancels tears and removes the hands of devourers from your life.
10. Tithing brings to an end every form of stagnation, barrenness and makes you dwell secured in God's grace

Beloved, tithing is not a law enunciated by the pastor, but a covenant principle in scripture that leads to the divine treasure room prepared specially for as many that obey God wholeheartedly.

Chapter 5

ARE YOU CURSED

Ye are cursed with a curse: for ye have robbed me, even this whole nation.

Malachi 3:9

As mentioned earlier, every instruction or law given to man by God has two sides, the blessing, and the curse. The blessing comes as a result of what has been done right and the curse as a result of what has wrongly been done. The curse does not just come to us without offence or breaking of the law, because the desire of God towards those that do His will is blessing, blessing, and blessing.

But those that feel they are no more under the law and are redeemed from its curse without doing the right thing get cursed. "*Christ hath redeemed us from the curse of the law, being made a curse for us: for it is written, cursed is every one that hangeth on the tree: that the blessing of*

Abraham might come on the Gentiles through Jesus Christ" (Galatians 3:13-14a).

Jesus truly took the curse upon Himself by shedding His blood on the cross. That way, one who believes in Him can be saved, but He never condemns or goes against the law. He said:

> **Think not that I am come to destroy the law or the prophets: I am not come to destroy but to fulfill**
>
> Matthew 5:17

Jesus went further to say:

> **And if any man hears my words, and believe not, I judge him not: for I came not to judge the world, but to save the world. He that rejecteth me, and receiveth, not my words, hath one that judgeth him: the word that I have spoken, the same shall judge him in the last day.**
>
> John 12:47-48

As stated in the scriptures, every word of God you rejec

for personal reasons will only wait for you on the last day. Jesus said, "I did not come to destroy the law or the prophets, but to fulfill all that has been commanded by my Father." The Lord Jesus approved tithing, including all other commandments, as stipulated in the laws of God.

> **Woe unto you, scribes and Pharisees, hypocrites! for ye pay tithe of mint and anise and cummin and have omitted the weightier matters of the law, judgment, mercy, and faith: these ought ye to have done, and not to leave the other undone**
>
> Matthew 23:23

Jesus knew tithe has its purpose towards God's work, so He, as the begotten Son of the Father, can never oppose it. Instead, Jesus rebuked the scribes and Pharisees of not giving attention to other matters that would make their tithing habit worthwhile. He said it is good that they devote themselves to all other areas of the law as they have done in the aspect of tithing and nothing should be underrated (Matthew 23:23)

A child of God that disagrees with the word of God because of doctrinal belief and fails to take instruction by the word written is cursed already. No one disagrees with the word of God and is counted among the redeemed; understand this very fact.

OPERATOR OF THE ORDER

Jesus Christ is aware of the significance of tithe to the smooth running of the Father's business for which He came. There is no reason why Jesus must stand against tithing because He was part and parcel of the arrangement in heaven. Tithing started 430 years before the law was handed over to Moses by God (Genesis 14:20). Moses and other fathers of faith kept the ordinance until Jesus came to apply grace to it.

Another reason why the Lord would not oppose tithing is that He is the Chief Operator of the new order as Priest forever. The tithe helps to take care of the Levites; the priests; the poor in the fold; the ministers of the gospel; to fill God's storehouse, and to honour Him for all the He has ordained man to be in the presence of His heavenly host. For believers to emulate every righteous act, the Lord gave a teaching approving the acts of the scribes and Pharisees.

> **For I say unto you, That except your righteousness shall exceed the**

righteousness of the Scribes and Pharisees, ye shall in no case enter into the kingdom of heaven.

Matthew 5:20

Righteousness will make you stay through with the word of God without seeking options or shortcuts of carrying out the word. The Scribes and Pharisees knew the law has it that if you borrow the tithe to pay on a later date, there is a 20% interest added.

They saw this as an additional burden. Instead, they preferred to keep tithing as at when due religiously. A whole lot of faithfulness was attached to their obedience of tithing, and noted by Jesus Christ as righteousness on their part.

Your righteousness and obedience to God must be tested to equate the righteousness of the Scribes and Pharisees before you can be ascribed worthy to enter the kingdom of heaven. Strive hard to do God's will.

THE PROMISE OF ABUNDANCE

Our God will never promise anything He will not do. If He is saying prove me now herewith, "...if I will not open you the windows of heaven...." (Mal 3:10)., it shows that there is an abundance of good things lying in wait for us all when the word of God is followed to the end. God never lies or says a thing and not bring it to pass; His word is sure.

The seed sown into God's ground can produce and bring forth good harvest. In like manner, the word of God can be sown to get harvest. Your substance that comes as a result of your income can also be sown into God's fertile ground for harvest. Prosperity and good success come as a result of the word of God you have taken inside of you.

> **This book of the law shall not depart out of thy mouth, but thou shalt meditate therein day and night that thou mayest observe to do according to all that is written therein: for then thou shalt make thy way prosperous and then thou shalt have success.**
>
> Joshua 1:8

Why God asked us to sow by giving our tithe, offering, seed and so on is not because He does not have enough, but because He needed us to walk in the abundance that He has promised us through Abraham.

He said to Abraham in the second part of Genesis chapter twelve, verse three, "...And in thee shall all families of the earth be blessed". There are rules, ordinances, and instructions that must be followed to get to this abundance.

Child of God, what manner of blessing do you want from your father in heaven? How do you want this blessing to be – big or small? You need to know the types of giving to engage in receiving what you want.

Chapter 6

GENEROUS GIVING

Any generous giving can become a memorial so that each time it is remembered above, a blessing is released to the giver down on earth. When you give, do not stand there waiting for a returned cheque. Take it as something released onto the Lord.

Your open hands towards members, servants of God and others in the faith is never lost labour, but wealth creation exercise which conforms with God's law of "it is more blessed to give than to receive."

TYPES OF GIVING

Five notable types of giving that attract different rewards to every faithful giver are in focus. For your knowledge, giving brings joy to the soul, and giving is living. It is like life and dead having the same four-letter words, but their activities are different from the other. Blessings are in levels, so is giving that causes the blessings to flow.

When you give God, what man will find hard to take from you, it is a clear indication that little or nothing may come to you as a blessing. God, all the time, needs the best from us so that He, in turn, can give us His very best.

No one will want to associate with low life, but extra valuable life that can offer a great blessing. If this is the case, then plan to give to life as a mark of investing in it. Your expectation should not be without anything planted. Giving is equivalent to sowing seed on the ground. Your harvest is the product of what you had sown. Know what to sow, how to sow, and when to sow it.

Worthy of note are these five kinds of giving, which can turn the situation around for every believer who does not question the word of God. Some say, "it never worked for me," and others say, "its old-fashioned doctrine, we are in the jet age." Child of God, take caution, the word of God is ever new and fresh for as many who abide in Christ.

(a) TITHES AND OFFERING

These twin giving belongs to God by covenant agreement He had with man from the foundation of the world. As earlier stated, it is bound on man to pay one-tenth of his earning, which is God's part to His storehouse, and where this is not done, it will be regarded as robbery

(Malachi 3:8-10).

When you give what belongs to God to Him, which is the tithe and offering, He returns riches, wealth and gives you the power to enjoy them all. Give God's portion to Him, and He will release your portion so that your labour may not be in vain through devourers.

> **Every man also to whom God hath given riches and wealth, and hath, given him the power to eat thereof, and to take his portion, and to rejoice in his labour; this is the gift of God.**
>
> Eccl 5:19

God allows you to enjoy the benefits of your labour whenever you release His part. The devourers are discomfited and turned from knowing your home address as you keep responding positively to God's command. The payment of tithe has benefited so many people who have taken the time to practise this principle, both Christians and non-Christians.

Beloved, never forget that when you tithe, you are saying, "I do not want the addition of death, devourer, poverty, lack, etc. in my kitty". Your tithe has the power to demobilise the devourer from acting against you. And as God starts working wonders in your life for this obedience of yours, the fire they have set against you opens and devours them. It becomes a case of the devourer being devoured.

The tithe is not crippling but crystalise. You cannot be a faithful tither, and God allows you to be crippled financially. Instead, it becomes more crystal clear that your belief is fixed like a coveted precious stone desired by all.

(b) SEED

> **Cast thy bread upon the waters: for thou shall find it after many days. Give a portion to seven, and eight; for thou knowest not what evil shall be upon the earth.**
>
> Eccl 11:1-2

The seed is a powerful sacrifice made by a person whose mind is fixed on God for a release of the desired need. This sacrificial giving can be from you to anyone anytime, anyhow and generously without restriction, but with the heart that you are doing it to the pleasure of the Almighty. *"And whatsoever ye do do it heartily, as to the Lord, and not unto men"* (Colossians 3:23). This giving has no boundary.

Look for every avenue to sow your seed, for no seed falls into a good ground without producing a harvest. Giving should be from a willing heart so it can attract a due reward from the righteous rewarder, Jesus Christ. A heart that is opened to give sends sensory signals to the heart of God, which draws Him to look down to the earth. This kind of giving is what the Lord refers to as sweet-smelling savour because it came from a pure heart, not just the huge nature of that sacrificial giving.

A seed that will touch the heart of God is a seed that can cause some pains to the giver. It is hard for those who do not have compassion and the heart for the things of God, to release their seeds for the gospel because their thoughts will be they have just lost a precious seed to the church and not to the Creator.

Release your seed with the mind of having your dealings with the Lord above, not with man. When your seed is sown is coming back to you, it will never be in the form it left your hand.

(c) FIRST FRUIT

What comes into your hands at the begging of the year s recorded as the first fruit, and it's set aside for God. It is an ordinance before the children of Israel that must be maintained for the storehouse of God not to lack anything.

> **And the feast of harvest, the first fruit of thy labours, when thou hast gathered in thy labours out of the field.**
>
> Exodus 23:16

Child of God, your first fruit stands as a booster to al other things which will be coming into your hand as the year runs by. Like tithe, the first fruit is a demand placed on man by God, because it is part of all that fills up the chambers of God's house (Neh. 10:37). Believers are enjoined not to forsake the house of our God for an reason.

Your first fruit is a factor of love that you can demonstrate towards the Lord. Common knowledge shows that what you love can gain more of your time and money than what you hate. Dedication to this ordinance is a sign that you are grateful for God's provision and grace upon your life. A heart directed towards God can give up anything for the sake of Christ Jesus.

(d) ALMS

Alms are given more by those who have love from the inside for other people's welfare. They feel what others are passing through and move further to render assistance. Their help comes in terms of material provision, financial and or spiritual help.

God is mindful of this kind of benevolence, as what they do to their fellow brethren is like it is done unto God according to the scripture. All alms givers have their benefits here on earth and eternal rewards prepared in wait for them in heaven.

Giving of alms should not be to those that had enough to throw away, but to the poor, maimed, the lame and the blind, so that God Himself can bless you for these set of people will not be able to repay (Luke 14:13-14). The reward for almsgiving comes from above openly.

> **That thine alms may be in secret and thy Father which seeth in secret himself shall reward thee openly.**
>
> Matthew 6:4

Your alms can become a memorial like that of the Macedonia church, which, though they had their difficulties, pains, and poverty, it never debars them from lavishly and willingly giving to support the ministers and work of God.

(e) VOW

Another area that needs to be mentioned for the records is the vow. Many believers fall victim of this because they are very good at making vows and not fulfilling them.

A commitment made with a firm promise to bring it to pass is known as one that has entered a kind of oath with another. In this regard, you are coming out openly to bind yourself with the Lord in a promise to do something that will never fail to be done. It is a declaration made by a person that must not break or not be abandoned. Religiously, it becomes sin before God when one vows without fulfilment (Deut. 23:21; Eccl 5:5-6).

If you walk out of what you promised to do, God frowns at it, and it has a way of working against the one that made the vow. A vow is a solemn promise to God in the presence of His people.

A vow may not just be about the cash you will give, but what you can do to please God. Commitment to release oneself to serve God in any condition with all you've got and to do all that He has instructed. A vow is a bond that remains binding until the person involved fulfils it.

> **If a man vows a vow unto the Lord, or swear an oath to bind his soul with a bond; he shall not break his word, he shall do according to all that proceedeth out of his mouth.**
>
> Numbers 30:2

Though God is going to forgive vow breakers who have repented and shown sincere concern for failure to redeem the vows, it is still not ideal that we indulge ourselves in this kind of habit. When we make a vow, enough level of honesty is required because vow fulfilled brings joy and blessing to the soul and honour to God (Deut. 23:21-23, Eccl. 5:1-7, Acts 18:18).

A vow is not just what you will do, but also what you have promised not to do to honour the Lord. Vows paid brings deliverance to the soul.

Chapter 7

REQUIREMENTS FOR BLESSING

Beloved, giving to God raises your financial profile, not God's as whatever you give was given to you by Him. The Bible says "For who maketh thee to differ from another? and what hast thou that thou didst not receive? Now if thou didst receive it, why dost thou glory, as if thou hast not received it?" Nothing is too big to give to God if you count all He has done and still doing in you. You are His project, and surely He will not forsake or leave you to frustration.

If you do not show the Lord how wise and intelligent you are, His grace for blessing never stops pouring on you. Blessing has been declared upon men by God through Abraham, but everyone's portion is predicated on personal activities. Above all, certain requirements turn on the blessing notes, and they are:

a. **Consecration**

Purity unto God is a standpoint for the flow of blessing from above. The channel of the overwhelming sea of good things will keep flowing as that man's total being is purified unto God. God feels honoured to make all things available for as many that seek Him with a pure heart. Man's link with the supernatural realm is through purity and holiness of the heart. Note this:

> **Then Hezekiah answered and said, Now ye have consecrated yourselves unto the Lord, come near and bring sacrifices and thank offerings into the house of the Lord. And the congregation brought in sacrifices and thanks offerings; and as many as were of a free heart, burnt offerings.**
>
> *2 Chro. 29:31*

Consecration causes acceptance of your offering, and acceptance opens the doors of blessings. Beloved, pursue holiness in all its entirety and then be ready for the outpouring of God's blessings. Without consecration at least to a level, some blessings will be very hard to access. Consecration is unavoidable.

b. **Follow Instruction:**

One can become a destroyer of his or her blessing if he/she refuses to carry out God's instructions. God said if you fail to bring your tithes and offerings you have robbed Him. And the book of proverbs said

> **Whoso robbeth his father or his mother, and saith, it is no transgression; the same is the companion of a destroyer.**
>
> Proverbs 28:24

God is our Father; anything He says is binding on us as dear children. Getting something from above requires the presence of God, when we steal from Him without any remorse, the repercussion is that we succeed in, destroying the source where the blessing flows. We may not realise its damaging effect at the beginning, because the drop comes slowly until it becomes very glaring. Instructions followed completes your joy.

c. **Wisdom**

One priceless tool one needs to procure Godly riches and blessings is wisdom. Creation does not relegate anyone, but some must be behind so that the sons of the

Most High can be above only. The Lord is happy when the children seek for wisdom to do His will on earth. God's wisdom is available for everyone willing to succeed.

> **Whoso loveth wisdom rejoiceth his father: but he that keepeth company with harlots spendeth his substance.**
>
> Proverbs 29:3

With wisdom, you can build on the source of blessing and know the right thing to do in a way it will look pleasing to the giver of blessing God.

d. **Pay your correct tithe**

Though tithing is not a means of getting to heaven, the facts remain that it's a Christian-based practice, which conforms to God's ordinances. It is undertaken by as many whose salvation is founded on the teachings of the gospel of Christ.

We are not paying tithe to enable God to feed well or live big, but to demonstrate our commitment to how much we can reciprocate His great love poured out for humanity. Brethren, not just paying tithe, but paying the correct tithe as at when due to God that makes the windows of heaven to open on us. Not paying the correct tithe is short-changing oneself from receiving the real blessing. Believe it or not, there are blessings tied to tithing.

e. **Faith**

One of the most needed elements in getting service to God rewarded is faith. Absence of faith places restrictions on divine manifestation. Scripture says

> ***Now faith is the substance of things hoped for, the evidence of things not seen.***
>
> *Hebrews 11:1*

If one must receive a blessing as desired, one must believe first even without seeing. Unlike the world, God wants His children to trust Him, nothing doubting, and then they have what they desired. In the eyes of faith, what is requested already delivered without delay? Faith sees what hope expects to get.

To appropriate enough blessing from the throne of all-sufficiency, faith must be seen working. Faith must show its work to attract a due portion of blessing. Faith is a magnetic force to secure heavenly blessings. Have faith enough to grab your blessing.

Chapter 8

CHARACTER AND OBEDIENCE

The third president of the United States of America, Thomas Jefferson, said: "Nothing can stop the man with the right mental attitude from achieving his goal; nothing on earth can help the man with the wrong mental attitude."

"A man's character is his fate" – Heraclitus.

Child of God hear this, what we often call destiny is our character, and since the character can change, destiny also can change. Life is like a river; it flows down channels finding its way along. A believer holds prayer in very high esteem, but prayer cannot change everything if the character is not in proper shape.

Anyone willing to change a bad character can, over time, become a transformed person producing visible results of good things in life. Note that the fact that a man is moving to high places in life doesn't mean fewer enemies are waiting for him there, but the character that follows him there is what matters. Check the character that goes with you.

What kind of personality do you put up when it comes to the things of God? When God is mentioned around you, how is your response? Do you tune into the spirit mode and put character aside, and you think it will make a suitable replacement as a balancer? No.

Many have been so occupied in our generation with the thoughts of going to heaven without any single trace of cordial interpersonal relationship with God inside of them They remain very aggressive, unapproachable, and in all the word of God is dull in their ears. Without character and obedience to God's basic laws for human co-existence there can be no manifestation of God's glory, blessing, and power.

As believers, we are not serving God because we wan someone to praise us, but all is about our desire to release our lives to the one who gives life. He has said in Ecclesiastes 12:13 that, *"Let us hear the conclusion of the whole matter: fear God and keep his commandments: for this is the whole duty of man".*

Some group of people in the history of Scotland calle

the Covenanters came together and entered a covenant saying, “we will have no king, but Jesus.” And you can see an old Scottish man shut his teeth and open the vein in his arm to take blood for the signing of the covenant.

Three hundred thousand of them gave their lives to make that covenant – we will have no king, but Jesus. How effective is your commitment to your service to God? Good character, with obedience to God's word, generates divine blessings.

There are sacrifices to pay when it comes to pleasing the Lord. Nothing appears glorious by wishful thinking. When you have good character and accompany it with obedience, the law of God will become very easy to follow.

Obedience, in itself, has a lot of blessings to offer to every true believer. Like a master key, obedience is capable of leading to the opening of so many unmerited doors of blessings. Great doors of success, greatness, and answers to prayers are waiting for a knock of obedience from someone. Make yourself available; you can be that favoured individual.

Necessary to say is the fact that faith is equally required to stay on to the word of God, and then, character and obedience are vital tools if one must harness the benefits thereto. It is a waste of effort and time if, at the end of the whole struggle on earth, nothing is achieved because of dirty character and lack of obedience to God's word.

All other forces that contend with man are obedient to the word of God. The Lord has said "I have made all things to work together for your good." Whenever we display good inside of us, we attract his goodwill that is made available towards all men.

To effectively do the will of God, you need Jesus Christ, who is the word himself, to control your affairs. Many today do not have Him; that's why it is effortless for them to flaunt God's order at the slightest provocation. Learn to follow God like a child, and it will be a simple thing to carry out his instructions any time without thinking how the flesh receives it.

CHARACTER AND OBEDIENCE

CONCLUSION

In the hollow of His hand, men derive abundant flow to fulfill their desires. The presence of God produces man's positive nature to life. We can never detach God from the affair of men and expect to present a better image of God.

Obedience to God is a commitment to do whatever He says. Hear what David, the King of Israel, said concerning the Almighty:

> **Thou wilt show me the path of life: in thy presence is fullness of joy. At thy right hand, there are pleasures forevermore**
>
> Psalm 16:11

A demand is placed upon lovers of God by Christ in the book of John 14:15, which says, "If ye love me keep my commandments". When God guides, you are safe. There is no success without the application of the word of life.

According to as his divine power hath given

unto us all things that pertain unto life and Godliness, through the knowledge of him that hath called us to glory and virtue.

2 Peter 1:3

Beloved, no child of God decides what rule or part of the word to obey and the one to discard. There is no part of Scripture that is obsolete to man; every word of God is valuable in this present dispensation.

To be a beneficiary is to be a word practitioner. Doing according to the word is opening doors of abundant blessings. Always be willing to do God's will that sets you above only and never beneath.

Shalom!

Notes

www.ingramcontent.com/pod-product-compliance
Lightning Source LLC
LaVergne TN
LVHW010118170826
845678LV00012B/2479